This journey is about
the words, but also
the feeling!

Philly, PA

TRAVEL BY HAIKU: VOLUMES 6 - 10

FAR OUT ON THE ROAD WITH FRIENDS

COMPILED BY
MARSHALL DEERFIELD

spread it

A FREEDOM BOOK

Published by A FREEDOM BOOKS

Copyright © Marshall James Kavanaugh, 2021

LIBRARY OF CONGRESS CATALOGUING IN PUBLICATION DATA
Kavanaugh, Marshall James, 1987—
Travel By Haiku: Volumes 6-10, Far Out On The Road With Friends
/ Marshall James Kavanaugh
p. cm.
ISBN 978-0-9984-2583-2
1. Kavanaugh, Marshall James, 1987— -Biography.
2. Authors, American—21st century—biography

Printed in the United States of America

contact@marshalljameskavanaugh.com
www.marshalljameskavanaugh.com

Contents

Preface

It was only a matter of time until the practice of writing haikus, which for me began as a personal meditation, would ultimately expand to a form of collaboration. This new collection of *Travel By Haiku, Volumes 6-10: Far Out On The Road With Friends* does its best to pay tribute to the community that one finds on the open road and the endless inspiration that is shared within such an intimate space of creative discovery.

The haikus printed here were gathered during a series of three road trips that took place between 2015 and 2016 with three individual groups of fellow rucksack revolutionaries and our main protagonist, Marshall Deerfield. The first, a roadrunner's ramble through the Big Bend region of West Texas with Augustus Depenbrock. Followed not too long after by a month-long jaunt up the Pacific Coast from Los Angeles to Seattle, stopping at every natural wonder along the way, with Shane Donnelly and Tara Lynn Faith Williamson. Last, but not least, a dive deep into the Rockies with Stephanie Beattie and Cameron Christopher Stuart, on the way from Taos, New Mexico, to the crown jewel: Glacier National Park in Montana.

The way it worked is while the tiny red clown car hurtled across dynamic landscapes of forest, desert, and ocean; its passengers passed back and forth a single notebook, each tackling a line and together creating a stream of haikus that described their collective experiences. As the authors alternated in clockwork fashion, passing the notebook from driver to shotgun to backseat, each writing only one line of the haiku, pausing for the last transcriptionist to begin the next sequence, the voice of the poem began to call out.

This last part to the surprise of each author.

What they wrote together was not only a decent, if sometimes absurdist, attempt at capturing the world around them, but also a demonstration of the unique cadence and assortment of motifs that developed with the progression of each journey. Sturdy as a Cascadian mountain or a 3000-year-old cedar, each motif stands alone as an ode to the roots beneath the moment. The collective voice of their own unique claim to the road orated from the tip-tops of each syllable into the valleys of deeper meaning.

Behind each haiku is a story. This portion of the book picks up right where *Volumes 1-5: Still Trippin' Across The States* left off: Marshall Deerfield is on the western leg of his first ever cross-country poetry tour expanding his understanding of the connection between magic and nature, and then only a year later he is living in New Mexico heading toward Montana, deepening in the roots of his surroundings. In this regard, the story follows a young poet growing wilder until, ultimately, he becomes the woods he sought all along. Further on, we as readers are faced with the question of where a haiku actually comes from. Who is the author? Is it actually the poet? Or is it the woods themselves?

These adventures took place during a time when Black Lives Matter was still expanding into a national movement from its initial outpouring in the streets of Ferguson and Baltimore where it sought to further address police brutality and systemic racism. It was written as the water crisis raged on in Flint, Michigan, offering a daily exposé of capitalism's failures and its collapsing infrastructure. As haikus were found in the pest-infested forests along the Rocky Mountain chain, nearby the Standing Rock Nation was issuing a call for indigenous peoples from around the world to come to North Dakota and help defend ancestral drinking waters on the Missouri River against the Dakota Access Pipeline. All this while a tempestuous election cycle spelled out just how much work we have left to do as individuals in America to counter white supremacy, corporate oligarchy, and climate change.

The warrior path, however, is not limited to the frontlines. In between battles, for some, there is often a need to find a patch of wilderness to regroup and recharge and plan the next course of action. The highly revered Santee Sioux poet and activist, John Trudell, says in his 1980 Thanksgiving Day speech:

"Our power will come back to us, our sense of balance will come back to us, when we go back to the natural way of protecting and honoring the Earth. If we have forgotten how to do it, or we think that it looks overwhelming, or think that we can never accomplish it, all we have to do, each one of us, an individual, is to go and find one spot on the Earth that we can relate to. Feel that energy, feel that power. That's where our safety will come. The Earth will take care of us."

Explored in this collection is a discovery of the meandering paths to mature and grow a greater sense of meaning from experiences found only in the woods. It captures those moments between the battles, when the spirit is encouraged to feel empowered again by the crashing tides of the ocean and the golden halo that surrounds the moon. It is shared as a way of honoring some of the sacredness we fight for, when we stand up against injustice elsewhere. The peace felt in nature. The beauty of community. The freedom all people should have to chase after joy.

Those familiar with the American Pops of Jack Kerouac, the blues-infused ku of Sonia Sanchez, or the travel fiction of Basho will see the parallels between the spirit of the road, as it was and as it is now: an ever-changing, undying wanderlust that brings people together across distances unknown until they are adventured, together. This collection offers a snapshot of all those collective wanders intersecting the contemporary highways of America even now as this sentence is written.

This experience of the road is told through the viewpoint of the Deerfield legend, but it reaches beyond that, even further, into the far out reaches of road that are still yet to be traveled. An invitation to join, and an update on both the beauty found in the outdoors and the effects of climate change on the natural world.

Let the history books reflect one day that all these artists and writers and poets and clowns held the road together, steering toward their dreams and reaching out for something bigger than their origins. Finding at the source of it all, rituals and ceremony to be recorded and then reused at a later date. Words that bubble up from the lips of a mountain stream begging for society's return to a greater relation with our mother planet. Learning that the journey to get there is only half the path to awakening. This book, like a vehicle, points the direction and revs its engine, fueled by each haiku, as it carries the reader toward the sublime only ever found in the stillness of Earth's deepest corridors.

Travel By Haiku is an affirmation. We all have this opportunity to find our woods and find the words to uplift what remains of the natural wildness that exists all around us, as well as the endless wilderness waiting to be cultivated within. I hope each page in this collection serves as a map to get back home again.

Marshall James Kavanaugh
Philadelphia, PA
March 2021

Introduction

I stuffed my backpack and guitar case in among the other belongings crowding the backseat: travel bags, a suitcase, a typewriter, a folding table and chair, boxes of books, framed photographs, stereo speakers, dream catchers, and a gray herringbone blazer hanging from the hook over the window for special occasions – never know when you'll come across a cocktail soiree! After some light rearranging and wedging of objects into all available crannies, I found there was just enough room to get comfortable.

I came to know that space well – one of contradictions: of rest and of excitement, of refuge and of exploration; at once a cramped enclosure and a threshold to ever-expanding vistas. Packed away back there, often-times drowsy, always cozy; I observed from the window the world soaring past, while up front Simian and Deerfield rattled on emphatically about philosophy, literature, past loves, future loves, the wind, the rain, the sun, the moon – no subject was too mighty nor too complex that the whirring apparatus of the road could not disentangle it. Or more than likely, my co-piloting cohorts could be heard intoning inspired gibberish, admixtures of awe and car-bound delirium when no logical utterance would suffice to ascribe meaning to the staggering sights before us.

"A mountain – ooh hoo!"

"Rainbow! Ba-hah!

"Why, would you look at that corn! I reckon that field must stretch from here to Shambala! Pu-ha-la!"

As the gentle rocking of the vehicle lulled me into a midday nap, their hollers served as the chorus to the amphitheater of my dreams. My haze of consciousness swirled with the crisp yellow of sunflowers flooding past under South Dakotan skies, notorious in their breadth and scope. One very well might find Humpty and his million shell shards reconstituted there among the clouds, not to mention the king's calvary decked out in fleece.

Somewhere on 90, between Missoula and Spokane, I awoke to Simian saying, "You know, sometimes I start to feel my voice shifting. Like suddenly I'm speaking from the voice of another driver. Or not even the driver – it's like each vehicle has a voice. And you can tell what it sounds like just looking at it. Something about that truck in front of us, just makes me wanna say," his voice now rising to a musical twang, "'Look it that truck over thar!'"

"Ya mean that truck thar?" Deerfield responded in kind, bouncing in his seat as his finger tapped the windshield.

"Yar, thar's the one. That un thar!"

"The green un?"

"Naw, the yaller un!"

"Har har ta har!"

And so on with idiot laughter rolling out the windows to be lost forever in those endless acres.

***

The road's a shapeshifter. We plunge through its bleeding landscapes like the western sun dripping into the sea. One day you're staring up the trunk of an 800-year-old Douglas fir, the next you're on a rain-drenched beach, using a rock to unloose a sabertooth from the jaw of a dead seal, bloated and morose on the Oregon coast. Given enough time, the driver enters a trance; the motor guides him past each successive mile marker. His fellow passengers too become enlisted, and soon we are all reciting poetry; Jo Simian up front with his outlaw guffaw and me in the back between spasmodic snores; Deerfield's hands all the while fast on the wheel, his eyes taking in everything from the highway paint shooting past like lasers to the steadfast glint of the moon.

As the land marches by, so too a parade of characters. A farmer tracing ancestry through potatoes, a ten-times-married man experimenting with pendulums, an Air Force veteran who built landing tarmacs in the deserts of Afghanistan grown lonely in civilian life, a San Francisco beach bum pirate in search of lost brothers, a German-Irish boozed-out poet moved to tears by a photograph: each soul an ambassador of this strange world we inhabit, representing its joys, its sorrows, its dreams.

And then us three – Deerfield, Simian, and Bandalini – rushing into the nearest burger joint, our appetites eager for something other than blocks of cheese and granola bars, setting up camp in a corner with notebooks spread on greasy tabletops (garnering odd looks from other customers, no doubt), penning lines of verse between mouthfuls of chili, careful not to spill too much sauce in the margins, sitting quietly for long stretches like monks recording sacred thoughts, then looking up in unison, and exploding into laughter.

But even our merry band of travelers was not immune to the never-tiring pulse of change. After our first night in Portland, we awoke to find the cartop canvas bag we used for storing belongings had been punctured and deflated. A thief in the night had gutted the bag and absconded with Jo Simian's luggage. Feeling a little low, he endeavored nevertheless to visit a thrift store that afternoon and replenish his wardrobe. But before he could, as if by fate's design, he received a phone call that same morning beckoning him home. His grandfather had taken ill and was possibly approaching his last days on this planet. Simian was on a flight back East that evening, wearing his herringbone blazer.

Some time later, Deerfield and I drove to a campground in Crater Lake National Park. With Simian gone I'd graduated to the front passenger seat. Before we got to the campground though, we had to travel a winding mountain road densely thicketed that night by fog. We could hardly make out a few feet of the road ahead. There was only fog and beyond that, nothing. It was as though the world had vanished and been replaced with fog. Certainly, the wide-eyed look on Deerfield's face suggested we had drifted into some liminal zone, a stranded place between space and time.

The fog seemed to contain restless spirits. They clamored one over the other, only to dissipate into nothing. I stared more deeply into that roiling mass but saw nothing but more fog buried within the fog. The road, the mountain, the night itself, all was swallowed and lost in the fog. It was impossible to imagine that somewhere out there past that impenetrable wall of vapors was a house in New Jersey where Simian sat at his ailing grandfather's bedside, listening to his labored breath; and elsewhere in New Jersey, my own parents, growing older, grayer, full of troubles. No – such thoughts were very far from our minds. It was only us, the car – the fog. And just beyond the edge of the road was an all-too-real drop down a sheer cliff face. We focused our efforts on the road ahead so as not be tricked by the spirits into untimely doom. Engaging in a kind of speaking meditation, we carefully made passage through the unfurling currents. "Easy there… easy there. Careful now. Woo! I tell you, we're either floating on cloud nine or else we've already flown out past that cliff and sunk down into the Land of Shades!"

Not long after that, pressures unique to my own life (matters best left for another story) beckoned me back East and, like Simian before me, I heeded the call. I bid Deerfield adieu under a neon donut shop sign in L.A., sorry and somewhat ashamed to abandon him like that. It seemed like an eon we'd been trekking together. It was strange to leave so suddenly, a phantom absorbed back into phantom mists. Sorry as I was, I knew Deerfield would do just fine. Already, he was starting to look angelic, a patina of sun having given his skin a healthy glow, coastal winds having massaged his hair into a crown of waves. We hugged and then stood there a moment, glowing. Everything glowed in that Hollywood sun – or maybe I'm remembering a scene from a movie.

Of course, this collection has nothing to do with me, or my memories, or a scene from a movie. It's about the trees, valleys, mountains, moon, and clouds. It's about the body in movement and the body at rest. It's about the wonder of imagination as it merges with the mystery of nature. And it's about the friends we make along the way! The poets, playwrights, gallerists, and yogis. But also the common man, the hardworking lout. The loaf-about. The drinker. The gambler. The devil. The priest. The lover. The saint. The myriad manifestations of Atman in adventure. And if there's one thing I've learned, an adventure is like the Hydra's head. When one comes to an end, twelve more spring up in its place. And so, in further adventures did I come to know the wanderers in these pages…

For the lonesome soul,
The Road is a companion;
We never go alone.

Andrew Galati
January 2021

Travel by Haiku

Vol. 6: **Desert Jesters Swim In Ancient Seas.**

with Augustus Depenbrock

A **wide** <u>open space</u>

empty except for two guys passing wind... through leaves.

You know why the
sand is so white?

they bus the old
people out here and
it swallows them up!

these dunes are all
their <u>white hair</u>.

Reds, Browns, Cerulean
sky sits high, stretching long
        paint mixed in heat.

       Sleeping black dogs lie
   in cool Terralingua shade
the cafe radio plays.

Steaming highway wind
   plucking vulture feathers
     a scavenger <u>poet</u>.

Beside
the white line

the **tie-dye**
scavenger
poet

harvests **dream**
catchers.

Bird wheels around sky
car circles around highway
            ALL are desert prey.

The high basin drains
        at sunset light floods purple
overflowing with bats.

            Spirits float across
        hot asphalt and desert sand
        singing
                electric.

Deep horizon line
    temperamental music box
        Full Moon is calling!

            Black scars in pink sand
        carry people across land
Cadillac country.

Dotted desert lines
    shuttle
            ranchers, hippies, heat
ALL love this dry land.

Three hawks
dancing

black against
the sky
the wind kicks
up dust.

We found a
bunch of

Lost Girls

trying to do **NYC
in the Desert**

sooooo

MARFA!

Hungry cops
trying to <u>catch</u>
<u>you</u> with your
pants down

prowling the
whole **two
blocks** of town.

Twenty feet
of pastel pink

it all disappears
and

the beauts
remain.

Quiet...

standing tall against

the **West Texas sky**.

Travel by Haiku

Vol. 7:
Scavenger Poets Tell Their Tales.

I could sit here
and
**write haikus
for the rest of
my life**,
but then what?

This is the Gulf of Mexico. To get here I had to drive through a literal ring of fire made up of oil refineries with their smoke stacks spewing blue, green, and red flames up into the heavens. It felt like driving through Mordor or some other land of constant manmade volcano. The air hangs heavy with sulfur and blight. Oddly these industrial feats are complemented by the largest marinas full of the largest fishing vessels I've ever seen, as if it weren't in the planning that these fruitful waters would want to be shared by anyone other than oil barons.

It truly seems like a hell on earth, but I finally make it to a small beach state park full of pelicans the size of bicycles flying and diving into the cool, blue waters coming up with their gizzards full of delight. During the night, the campsites were all full, so I skipped the tent fee and slept in a Walmart parking lot with beachfront property and watched the sun rise in these pretty pinks and yellows. Now I'm enjoying the small island vibes of the quiet sea. Texas is a funny place, but the people are real nice always with something friendly to add. It's only 9:00 a.m. but already close to 80 degrees.

I love these drives through the middle of nowhere. Stopped to grab some tail feathers off of a dead wild turkey. The thing was huge and still smiling. As I walked back to the car I found two feathers from a red-tailed hawk as well. Seems like I'll be entering Austin with some extra magic on my side.

Mellow vibes

A little retreat into
an Austin oasis

reggae   ghetto
blaster is full
throttle.

Austin is like this. It's how you get stuck here. You round the corner and there's a big spiral of pennies on the sidewalk. And then you stay there for like seven years picking up all of the pennies one at a time, seeing all the fortune you've acquired, but still feeling like a vagabond.

And then when you're like halfway through, another man comes around the corner and says, "Excuse me, sir. Do you have any change?"

You make a gesture to the ground and say, "Man, the streets are filled with it!" And then just like that he bends down and takes over picking it all up.

Morning view:
buttes
on the horizon
wild flowers
blowing in the
breeze.

Tonight, the Scorpio Moon rose with a white squall in the middle of nowhere, West Texas. Sheets of rain so thick across the windshield, we can barely see the road as we drive through going 20 mph in an 80 mph zone. The two tornadoes set down, feeding flash rivers and lightning brighter than day. We crawl through with white knuckles and exit the other side into a flat, plain topography letting the cloud cover clear, and out of thin air bursts that Queen of Cups, that Kali Destructor, that grave trickster of the lowlands, that babe in the sky being coy and shy after I first spot her with my eye and point up to her, hiding again behind a smaller set of clouds now, but eventually coming out fully to play with the wind, still raging at her backside and lighting up the whole horizon line with Mars rising now too, blaring red from the opposite end of the now completely clear, big sky nighttime amphitheater.

Grounded in desert
wildlife, sun salutation
flowing in the breeze.

Golden eagle calls
the sun sets
through the
window
wasps buzz in the night.

Well, Gus and I ford the Rio Grande and enter into Mexico. We follow the donkeys and pickup trucks into town, braving the 90 degree hot sun heat, and end up in a bar that is a little beyond the other two more touristy restaurants.

I step up to the bartender and order two beers and two shots of tequila, and all seven other people in the bar go quiet. I can feel their stares as the bartender pours our shots and serves our beers. Gus squeezes lime around the rim of his can of Tecate and sprinkles salt on the back of his balled-up fist. All eyes are on us as we cheers our shots and down them.

I stumble back and Gus lets out a yelp. Then everyone yells and rushes forward to pat us on our shoulders. I turn to the guy sitting next to me and say, "¡Salud!" and he nods his head and runs out the door and the next thing you know he's driving up to the front door of the bar in a Dodge Caravan and there's a whole mariachi band, all with sombreros, spilling out of it and into the bar and then they're serenading us singing loudly and we're ordering more shots and more beers, this time for everyone, and then the local cowboy comes by and we're all riding donkeys and the Sierra del Carmen is glowing red in the late afternoon.

The two other Americans in the bar come over and tell me, "I guess you two really brought the party." The whole town is there and we're feeling quite glad. The next closest town is 180 miles away and I can feel the isolation and I want to do something about the poverty, but for now it's a good first taste of the countryside in ole' Mexico. Quite a scene they have there in the border towns. It's too bad U.S. Customs closes at 6 p.m. otherwise maybe we'd stay even longer.

Red **desert sunset**
      carry the heat
         far away

bring the **night time** cool.

Two communities bridge two nations at the *Voices From Both Sides Festival* at the border of Texas and Mexico, in a town called Lajitas, with bands playing back and forth on both sides of the river. There's people swimming and throwing footballs back and forth, as well as free food and tons of family entertainment. All of this was organized to reopen a border closed after 9/11 and to reestablish the economic ties between these two towns that used to rely on each other's support in the middle of the desert.

There's country folk, salsa, mariachi, tacos, dancing, a long snake of shaking hands, and people walking back and forth freely between this border of semantics. It's a protest in the form of celebration.

One town split down the middle, when the U.S. Border Patrol closed down the border in 2002, now reunited for the third year in a celebration in the desert heat, an ultimate *Fiesta Protesta*, converging in the Rio Grande.

Families, friends, and former co-workers reconnected.

Music plays from both sides like a battle of the bands, but it's not a competition, it's all collaboration. Something as simple as crossing a river deemed illegal and the masses in response wading that river, showing they want their dual-nation community back.

Border Patrol is there. The news is there too. But this isn't a battleground. It's a humble block party.

They sure ain't kidding
when they say *New* Mexico
whole other country out here!

White lines drawn in sand
a vision without contrast
                except for blue sky.

Landed **on the moon**
        followed ripples in the dust
                perceived endless space.

I just passed five individual one-mile-long trains, and there are cows roosting on each side in these large, open plains, and I swear I saw a group of gazelles grazing behind one rancher's gates, and it reminded me of how while I was in Big Bend, I couldn't get over how lush it was, and all the green made me think of what Africa must look like somewhere near the hills of Kilimanjaro, and I kept saying to myself, "desert rainforest," and then add to that today I explored an alien landscape only it was actually something that shouldn't be so foreign since we all come from it in some way, the womb of this Mother Earth, and I've never seen it before at least not at such depths and not so crystallized and beautiful.

I'm on my way to Santa Fe because everyone said, "Skip Roswell and go straight to Santa Fe!" I have to say, I was a little let down by Roswell but also surprised by how much of a town it was and the thought crossed my mind, while I biked around the residences and a strip of hand-carved alien statues, passing a sculpture dedicated to Goddard, who used to launch rockets there in the 20s, of what a weirdo artist community would look like settling there wearing pink hair and googly eyes and building a cardboard spaceship and maybe setting it all on fire with some rocket fuel.

I'm distracted though with these ideas I had while in Carlsbad Caverns of building a light installation down among those stalactites and reading poetry out into all that natural reverb echoing back to me a delayed out dream soliloquy and maybe having an Arkestra perform in the background so it would truly be prolific, but that'll have to happen later because right now I'm enjoying whatever planet I'm on surfing into Santa Fe on the San Francisco trail, which signs say is historic.

Here I am, take me to your leader and bring me to your artsy dive bars in a basket of old laundry and cowboy hats.

How could a man obsess

about rhino horns when **stalactites exist**?

I'm embarrassed to say, but in a bathroom down in Carlsbad Caverns, I think a penny fell out of my ass. It'd be more reasonable to say it somehow hopped out of my pocket and into my underpants, but that would take away the magic. I'd like to think this is the next step of the penny meditation I've been practicing for more than a year. Maybe soon I'll be laying golden eggs.

A dog with pink sunglasses walks by, stops, and looks at me. This guy wearing a pink backpack comes up and says, "Joe, is that your business? Is that your business? No. No, it's not." And they walk away together.

The desert makes people weird. But what if I'm weirder than the desert?

After all the Santa Fe bars and cafés get me down because of how expensive everything is, I'm biking back to my hostel and this psychedelic old man who looks like he is twisted on something bikes past me going the other way, with his hand pointed for me, held over his head in this weird hanged man way, pointing across the street for me to look to my left, and so I look, and there it is, the Counter-Culture Café, where all the punks must be, though closed till morning.

A lone coyote:

jester **in a dire
land**

for him, though:

peaceful.

Moon   architecture

grounded on a
mountainside

the Earthships
nearby.

Saw plenty of flying saucers today, but last night I sat over a campfire with some other dream punks (I'm serious, they put out an album called "Dream Speak" in the 90s), and I tripped over the fact that we're all aliens in this ancient land.

Take a left at the
100-headed Buddha
and get lost in
red rock.

As the second leg of my trip comes to an end, I've been waking up these past few mornings with such big feelings of gratitude. With leg three, which involves another poetry tour, this time up the West Coast, beginning in a little under a week, I find myself at the penny arcades of Mesquite, Nevada, in a position to gamble away all of the pennies, nickels, and dimes I have found on the streets of our country. Double or nothing, they say. I shout "Puhala!" and put two pennies on 42 Black and the good fortune awaits either way.

West Coast, I'll be upon you soon! Ready yourselves for some jestful unicorning and pretty ridiculous good vibes. Can't wait to see what new stories we craft together out of the thin air of our imaginations.

Spiraling out is
the mind of a
Dream Poet
standing in
sunshine.

Back to California, land of my favorite sunsets, after about two months on the road and five months away. Last time I left this place, the whole sky lit up like it was on fire with that blood red color of the southwest sand reflecting off the white mountains of Joshua Tree, turning them purple. Now, upon my return at the same very point of the road, the sun greets me in the same very way and a two-mile-long train rides by giving it some solar reception.

Well, **back on I-10 heading to L.A.**

Can't wait to see the ocean!

Reunite with the Snake Priestess and Planes Drifter. They offer the illusory sounds of their band *Many Mansions*. Play a show at a place called *Moon Manor* with a bunch of moon goddesses and powerful spirits. Read lines about the muse and riff on that time I howled at the full moon in San Francisco. Everyone talks in transdimensional linguistics and at a certain point we reach new wavelengths. They make a human sacrifice of me and cut my still-beating heart out to feed to the audience.

I vibrate so hard I pass out in a little cuddle puddle of dance happy zen lunacy. Wake up in the morning and eat some oranges from the orange tree growing in the backyard. Listen to talk of community and gatherings and radical transformation. Getting ready to travel to Ojai or "Oh Hi!" as we say. A great greeting among such mighty creators.

To sit on a rock and watch

the sea.

There's nothing any

more

pretty.

As I drive into Oakland, with the full moon guiding my vision, I can't even tell you how much emotion I feel. It is like a long migration home. It feels like driving through a dream, into a dream, and once getting here, finding a dream. I still have 2-3 weeks of this book tour in front of me, but so beautiful to be back in this place where I make my new residence.

Oh, Cali sunshine
        lay it on me, sweet baby!
your warmth is **DIVINE**.

        Patchwork clouds of fog
        houses nestled on a hill
peaceful bay morning.

Went to Davis. Went to Sacramento. Sold some books. Sold some typewritten poetry. Added new rocket ship adjustments to the Toyota Yaris. Landed on the universal universe, a pleasant place with psychedelic birds and tons of toddlers.

Got on the road again. Passed YOLO. Passed the green orchards and the burnt out grass. Set a trajectory for planet Muladhara. Going to orbit its Buddha-holes and collect the headwaters. Headed to Mount Chakra. Mount Shasta! Going to find the goddess there and drink up.

The poet chops wood to keep **the inner fire** <u>burning with zen</u> joy.

Cosmic sunsets in Bend, Oregon, before a **backyard jamboree**.

Played in Bend. Watched a sunset that was twelve shades of purple. Got back on the road and took a dip in the Bagby Hot Springs below Mount Hood. Met the prudest nudist. Emerged a unicorn. Listened to the bird synthesizers hanging in the tall redwood trees and chippy chipmunks scurrying about my feet. At some point we write collaborative haikus. Now we're on the road again. Playing Portland. The next two nights are to be full of sweet dreams.

Roll through Portland. Find the Naked Bike Ride. Find the Pride Ride. Find the weird vibes. Hang at *Xhurch*. See a dream laborer create a dream exhibition out of raw and virtual materials. Create some dream poetry of our own. Have high whimsical conversation. Start Oculus Rifting. Wake up and start busking. Tempt the early afternoon brunch crowd. Have little luck with that so change spots and create a TAZ in an abandoned lot. Attract the vagrants, the travelers, the kids kicked out of bars. Write haikus about the sunshine. Meet a couple traveling from D.C. Get commissioned to write some poetry (finally!):

East Coast convergence
On the West Coast (best coast?)
Following our hearts.

Write a birthday poem and am hugged, dearly. Spread the wealth and buy a zine from another starving writer working the streets.

Move onto a show at *Human Body Flesh World*. Play a psychedelic set that is just the right amount of magic. Read a poem that we all wrote by the campfire, passing a notebook round and round. Elaborate a little. Where it is needed. Feel the posi vibes. Sell some books. Trade some inspiration. Feel gratitude and abundance.

The **blues and greens** of Oregon **mesmerizing** in saturation.

Go to a Noise BBQ. Hear about the unicorn bike ride happening as part of Pride. Watch a clown / wizard perform on circuit-bent toys while heckled by drainbows. Laugh ever harder. Feel like I just might be crazy enough for this town.

Ride up the highway to Olympia. Pass Mount Hood. Pass Mount Rainier. Speak out loud my ramblings for the romance I feel toward these endless mountains. Drive into town and drink again from the fountain. I'm told at some point in the night again that I belong here. Tell them later that this is one place where I'll retire. Feel the transient vibes. Swim in the upbeat melancholy.

Play a show to the passing flow.
Drink the blood of Mount Rainier.
Become a unicorn and speak some
political, beaten street vibrations.
See old friends all the way through.
Dream a "hell yeah!" vision of what
have you. Feel appreciated and
desired. Smile. Sleep. Breathe.
Excitement renewed.

The **Seattle sun
setting**,   reflecting,
        on Mount Rainier from afar.

                Up on Capitol Hill
c i t y   p s y c h e d e l i a
        melting pot (over)flowing.

Last night marked the end of a saga. End of a very short era if you want to get really dramatic. It was our last planned performance on this dreamy tour up the West Coast and through our collective imaginations. Again, I'm at a loss for words in expressing how grateful I am for being given so many opportunities to show my work and collaborate with the ethos of each community I've been invited to enter.

Over the last few months, I've met so many new faces and heard so many amazing stories, all the while repeatedly being inspired by the creative efforts of our generation. I feel like every day I've fallen head over heels in love with something in the moment, whether it be with a woman, or a song, or a mountain, or the ocean, or the air, or just some passing phenomenon on the highway. I've been turned on and the dial has been turned up.

Now, it is with many good vibes that I make the slow but steady descent back into my humble new home of Oakland, California. Sitting near Pike Place in Seattle, overlooking Mount Rainier, I can only think how happy I am to be back on this side of the continent and so close to this endless adventure.

Sailed on a ferry today watched **Mount Rainier grow** larger by the sea.

To be free and lost

one of life's
many wonders

here in now,
wild-eyed.

54

Travel by Haiku

Vol. 8: **Tree Clowns Climb High, Onwards & Outwards.**

with Shane Donnelly and
Tara Lynn Faith Williamson

Alive and gliding
along sharp bends
in the road.
Who knows
where
we'll go?

The car
packed so
tight
our minds are
forced to expand

**onward &
outward.**

Douglas firs lifting

buzzing
bliss
waves stimulate
at peace with
motion.

Why Did The Tree Cross The Road?!

I don't know;

Ask the Lumberjack.

Order of the
Snake Priestess

**magic in the
redwoods**

Sacred Bums

posing as clowns.

Sun pulling car
through snaking roads
surrounding streams,
my eyes overwhelmed.

Mountain river soul
emerald dreamscapes
paint my mind
the clouds all hiding.

Arrive forever

Hallelujiah-ay-ya-ay!

be still and
lie there.

Awakened
Conscious
navigator of the
soul
lights,
color,
action.

Green so green it **cries**
a magic carpet
disguised
wilderness holds us.

Three travelers brave
no pathways left
unexplored
mystery prevails.

Into the unknown darkness falls on our space trip **we light up inside.**

Hell yeah! **Smoke that weed!** the wisdom is in the trees smoke that far out tree!

Smoke that high wisdom unlock your **<u>holy sky mind</u>** voices of reason.

Evergreen forest
covered in the sun's sweet light
expansive delight.

Cloudless ocean sky
cosmic comics passing by
the road getting lost.

Smoke town!
Cigars! Beer!
signs passing in the distance
instantaneous life!

Planes Drifter drifts and

slumbers

upon fallen logs admiring the sea.

**Adrift
on driftwood**
soar like
woody
woodpecker

into the
cosmos.

Nothing is absent

eyes open to simple truths

welcome the frontier.

Zen loony **driving the lunatic** on the loose freedom incarnate.

Cascadian buttes
loom large as
the light dwindles
life finding its way.

Ambient beach band
filling our space ship
with songs
these **beats**
drop so fresh.

The same
freakin' crow

every mile marker

shaman
in disguise.

A <u>shaman</u> <u>in flight</u>. **messenger** of the **divine** soaring through the sky.

Ancient melodies
from trees,
haunted night spirits
amongst us and within us.

Lie down and listen
to the sound the water
makes
flowing down the hill.

Feel crazy sensations amongst loud formations

living,

breathing,

earth.

A lake so
blue that

jumping in feels
like falling

down into the sky.

Trusting in
the plunge

**the cold sea,
mother's body**

she births me
once more.

Volcanic Bellies

water so cold
that it stings

an anomaly.

Annointed in
love
**we spring
from** the
headwaters
joyous and
alive.

Birthdays
come and go
but things
continue to
grow
making life
special.

Maintain
sis-star-hood
the green
goddesses stand tall
echoing love light
**(ancestral
delight).**

The trail is endless

infinite can be
chill too

take **a walk
and see**.

Journey Endlessly

heading toward that perfect home.

Destination:

Free.

Travel by Haiku

Vol. 9:
The Plot Thickens, Connection Deepens.

Well, **just found another penny** in the **hot springs** today.

We're still all rich, fishies!

I sweat with my Taos family. Brothers and sisters of the heart. The Clown Baron and Lakes Whole Lakes, visiting from New York City, join in. We share this earthly womb while our grandmothers, placed in the center of the lodge, burn bright. Everyone calls me brother or nephew or grandson. Everyone is relearning this sacred right. Even those that have it deep in their bloodline.

The time is ripe for it. We all have relatives with cancers or addictions. We all care about the next seven generations. All of us send energy and protection to the peacewalkers of the Standing Rock Sioux Tribe in North Dakota.

I sweat with my ancestors. Coyote howls and Red-Tailed Hawk flaps her wings in front of me. Deer whispers her curiosity for the world and tells me of her general modesty. The burning stones in the middle remind me of Druid rock balances. In the complete dark, their faces come to me laughing and smiling.

At one moment, so many voices are talking, I can hardly understand them, though I know they are talking to me. At another, wisps of light gather in my periphery and shoot back and forth every which way. Every time my heart beats, I see red in my eyelids. But now and then it's blue and green.

I sit generally still and brace for the sea that washes over me. Other times I'm shaking. I'm dancing.

I sweat with my elders. There's a lot to sweat out. More than I thought was possible. But my elders guide me. They share water and tobacco with me. They hold me and sing songs for me.

Initially, I panic in the extreme heat. I panic from the inability to breathe in the hot steam bath air. Eventually, I realize my safety, my comfort, and all of my family here. I let go of my fear, and my body becomes the ground. With each round it becomes easier.

Four rounds we go. Four rounds of absolute heat. One for every direction.

Some of us have been fasting all week. Others need to leave and sit outside before the ceremony is complete.

I wonder what we look like from outside. I wonder if they can hear our muffled voices. I wonder if they too hear all of the spirits being raised.

When we exit the lodge, the first thing I do is look up. My eyes tuned into the dark, I see so many stars. I see our ancestors. They glow brightly still. It's as if we raised them with our songs.

Like everywhere in Taos, a ceremony is followed by a feast. We dine around a large table. We get to know each other more deeply. The food tastes even better after our collective journey. Abundance is appreciated with gratitude.

I feel lighter than air. My ride home, I practically fly there. In my sleep, I dream a thousand dreams, and they're all about my growing family.

The earth offers gifts
abundance at
rainbow's end
revealed by the storm.

Not sure where we are
     seems like **it's Colorada**
          those jagged peaks soar.

The ancients were here
windows open to old worlds
  NOW *the ancients sleep.*

         Desert, late summer
blooming mesas full of life
     trickster on each peak.

I'm familiar with driving and seeing Crow on every fence post, but it's been a while since I've flown along his path. Soaring across the highway when we pass. The way the sky changes at sun down when it has more room to express itself. How Rocky Mountains are actually quite rocky when they begin to populate the horizon. Passing towns have signs like "historic" and "preserving the West" with pictures of cowboys and yet there's only 100 years since their destiny manifest. I begin to see sunsets followed by sunrises. Days fulfilled to the full extent.

Fox greets us at the first campsite outside of Durango, Colorado. He stares nonplussed into the headlights waiting for us to make our move first. When we remain stunned, he moves back to his lean-to stores. A pile of packaged meat, robbed from some wayward wanderer. Fox carries off ham, ribs, turkey wing, one at a time. His bushy tail sailing behind him especially pompous.

We decide on a campsite less occupied, a little farther down the road. There's a feeling of darkness in the night, but we seem pretty much untouched by it. In the morning, Fox transforms back into his human form, comes and collects money for the campsite. He has a bit of a Southern drawl and is generally good-humored.

We see Coyote in the road. Several times. He's snooping after Wild Turkey. Later on the trail in Mesa Verde, Wild Turkey leaves behind his tail feathers for us to gather. I find Hawk's feather there as well.

The trail to the pictoglyphs is one of wonder. We drift through ruins, along canyons hundreds of feet deep, with bird faces and elder faces set in the stone all waving at us.

Mule Deer comes and visits our camp in the morning. She realizes we're friendly and invites her newborn fawn into our company. And then her sister follows her there too. Turkey Vulture circles above. Desert alive and well. Mysteries untold beginning to tell themselves.

The ancients visit our dreams. They visit our conscious conversations. We talk of existence and the story we all tell of being human. We envision the effect of humanity on the ecosystem. We express intelligence is probably not humanoid but rather a much larger system. Aren't moons intelligent? Aren't whole planets? If intelligence were to grow to its full potential, wouldn't it want to go some place it couldn't be found? Save itself from the primitive reaches of our warlike nations and go underground?

Some say,
Life's a beach

Deerfield says,
Get lost in it
and ***enjoy the***
view.

At the Great Sand Dunes, I climb over thousands of feet of sand. I lose my breath several times. I encounter my fear of heights even more often. Walking along the ridges of these sandy peaks. Looking out at panoramic views of mountains and plains all around us. I've never driven on such a straight, flat road before driving on the one that took me here. Three hours and not a single turn or change of scenery through the San Luis Valley.

The Dunes blow in the wind, and I follow them with my eyes into endless wonder. Laughing at the human tendency to see big things and decide to climb them. Our ape minds still wishing they never came down from the trees and the views they offer.

Simple moon landing

a bum clown
lost in the
dunes

gravity
s t u m b l e s.

On the way to the Rocky Mountains, I witness whole forests depleted. Ponderosa pines normally bright red with sunshine, turned gray as the life is sucked right out of them. Standing like zombies amidst their dying relatives. Shells of a corpse.

The trees are dying from something called pine bark beetles. These little beasts are going on parade in the summer haze. The pine bark beetles have always been an issue for these forests. They're not a foreign invader. The difference between then and now is global climate change.

The pine bark beetles need a three day freeze to keep their eggs from living in any special quantity. That hasn't happened in a decade. It's left these forests unchecked. Pine bark beetle populations are sweeping the landscape, feeding on the sap of the trees for miles in every direction.

Imagine death. Death is not some grim

reaper. Death is the gray carcass of a dead tree that no longer breathes out oxygen. Now drive through it for more than an hour. A hefty tinder box the size of an entire mountain range that spreads across our midwestern horizon, waiting for a lightning strike that sets off an untamable apocalypse.

As an eco-activist, I never thought a forest's demise would come from inside of it. These pine bark beetles are unlike any bulldozer or logging caravan. Chaining yourself to a tree to protect it has no use if the tree is being eaten alive from within.

The dead forests continue from the bottom edges of Colorado all the way up through Wyoming. Everywhere where the alpine forests were supposed to freeze and haven't in a decade because of the climate changing. Three-quarters of the forests dead. Sometimes more. The chaos looking so much different from last year's forest fires in Yellowstone or Yosemite. Wherein forest fires are usually complemented by green, new growth in a little under a year, these zombie husks of former trees seem to hold stubbornly onto the ground they claim. The ground dead too, not receiving any of the life giving nutrients stuck in each trunk.

As we drive through the miles of wreckage, all of our hearts ache. We find free wood and a natural spring in a town outside of the entrance to the national park. Both become part of our ritual:

Burn wood. Expel beetle from the forests. Drink water. Expel black snake from our rivers.

Speechless.　　　Lost for words.
　　Mountains unfathomable.
　　Rocky **Mountain high**.

　　　　　The peaks of mountains
scales a dead giveaway
　　　　stone dragons sleeping.

High in the alpine
　　　　　mind **blooms**
　　　　　with wildflowers
　　special kind of bliss.

In the park we find Elk. Elk Bull has deep, black eyes the size of whole universes. We stare into those eyes and see ourselves reflected. He parades his women in front of us. They swim in Dream Lake. Then he stands upon the path. The wind blows and he stamps his feet. He shows us his antlers. His broad chest. He spits at the ground and howls. A show of strength. But Elk Bull's howl is more like a whistle. His whistle is welcoming. Accepting. He moves back to his grass meadow. He lies down. Enjoying all of the attention he receives from the passing hikers.

Pure golden meadow atop the alpine trail
nothing but the *breeze*.

The Grand Tetons are surrounded by more dead forests. Everywhere we drive, this seems like the future of our world. We all comment that perhaps we'll never see a full pine forest again in our lifetime. Even with pines growing quick, this is the obvious collapse of an ecosystem.

The Tetons look over this disarray. Their heads high in the clouds. Already we had started to see these rocky mountains as stone dragons, frozen by time. But the Tetons rise higher than we can even believe. And with no foothills! Seemingly springing from the ground itself. Their purple shoulders arched over green meadows below. Glaciers that reflect the sun and form lakes like oceans.

From our campsite we hike into a wilderness filled with Grizzly Bear. His scat and claw marks along the trail. But though we sense Bear, he does not cross our path. Instead on Hermitage Point we find the Hermit. A lone, elder Elk who regards us from afar with subtle interest.

We stare at him as the sun sets. He stares at us and nods peacefully. Eventually he continues on into the forest and we continue on toward the lake.

At this end-of-the-trail peninsula in the water, we see the sun set over the Tetons. And while its final glow is still settling in the western horizon, Moon at her fullest begins to rise upon the peaks in the east.

The three of us are silent. Our minds mystified. Both forces glowing so bright in the sky. All of it reflected upon this glacier lake. Night and day collide. And the glaciers on those peaks lighting up electrified. There is no other course of action but to meditate.

The Moon and The Sun command it.

A good friend once said:

"The **moon speaks for** the glaciers."

Earth hardly listens.

Melted glacier lakes
visionary reflections
        Grand Tetons rising.

Clouds swallow them whole
peaks   peeking   through
                in shadow
    Snake River drifts by.

Beast moving mountains
portrait of the buffalo
        'merica's heartland.

The next day we drive into Yellowstone. Waterfalls and rivers galore. Abundance that shouts. A park larger than Rhode Island and Delaware combined. Steam vents and dried lava pools. Some places appearing like hell on earth, and yet beautiful. Prismatic pools. Sapphire pools. Geysers that shoot high into the air. Everything bubbling with living friction.

We hike to the Boiling River. There we descend into two waterways. Both of them exhaustive in their extreme properties. One ice cold. The other boiling hot.

It's been two years since the last time I sat here. Not much has changed. I feel my skin scorched and soothed. Mind leaving body. Words come to me direct from the source. Haikus later to be written down in notepads. Ode to a boiling lobster of a human in such a strange ecology.

An ice cold **river**
meets a river on fire
what tranquil
balance.

River canyons grow
time
digging away at rock
life veins
of the earth.

We leave Wyoming. Enter Montana. In the middle of the night, we find the Missouri River headwaters. This sacred river, now receiving so much attention from its protectors downstream at Standing Rock in North Dakota. We figure we'll camp here and send a little prayer down the river from our fire.

But before we know it, we are driving up to this towering behemoth. A factory lit up in orange light like the tower of Mordor. Just half a mile beyond the state park, this concrete plant stands blaring mechanized sounds of nature being destroyed. Oil. Smoke rising. Train cars pulling away marked with hazardous waste. It absolutely terrifies us. No camping near this obvious polluter.

But why so close to the river? Why so close to the Three Forks where several lifelines jut to life? Seems like catastrophe waiting to happen. We get out of there quick, maybe with a plan to return on our way back with some daylight.

Eventually, we hit Missoula. Small mountain town. But with similar currents to the Pacific Northwest. Real live tramps. Mixing with hippy college students. So much color and diversity of spirit. And just in time for a week-long poetry fest.

I'm tempted to never let this trip end. In the night, I almost drive us to Seattle. Not paying attention to the GPS. Too engaged in a story about the Clowniverse. Things can go anywhere. Sometimes time just seems to fly by.

Now our trip takes a different rhythm. Settling down in a cabin at the entrance to Glacier National Park. Time to write. Time to vibe. Time to take a shower that's not in a hot spring on the side of a river.

114

Cabin on
a lake

perhaps
the perfect retreat

to **take
it easy**.

I've noticed my outwards appearance begin to reflect my surroundings. My black t-shirt growing bleach-stained roots. A button down printed with tiny tents among pine trees. A sweater with quilted fabric weaving it all together. And a new jean jacket camouflaged in ferns.

Certainly normal for a Dream Poet. This reality blending into a collage of natural wonder. The body becoming just another piece of the forest.

Blue, a fellow haiku poet from Philadelphia, told me at the beginning of this crazy adventure over two years ago:

"Find your woods, Deerfield!"

I always took it to mean,
"Find your *self*".

Never realized the self could ultimately become *The Woods*.

Encountering bliss

heaven's
colorful
repose

**paradise
unfolds**.

I see parts of the park that weren't open the last time I came here. I see things I'm not sure aren't just a painting or some other illusion of clouds and fog.

Three days in Glacier National Park and I return to the hike that I took in the park two years ago, when I first ventured into this wilderness fresh from Philadelphia joined by Antonio Bandalini and Jo Simian on my first road trip across the country.

The trail is to Avalanche Lake. A turquoise blue wonder beneath melting glaciers seated high above on freshly scarred peaks. The hike starts out in an old growth grove of cedar trees. Some 1,000 years old. Some older.

Walking amongst these elders reminds me of the many hikes with redwoods and Douglas firs that I've taken in the last two years since that first road trip. Things I hadn't even imagined existed yet, that first time through.

There's something about trees that old. They remain sacred through multiple human generations. Here are trees that the Kootenai and Salish people, indigenous to this area, revered as ancestors several centuries ago; stewarding their growth and passing on those traditions to their relatives today.

I feel like I'm arriving home. Not to any place in particular, but more to that feeling my heart gets when communing with giant trees of ancient eras.

And here I am standing in awe, when I notice a little sign next to one of the elders. On it is a drawing. Written beside the drawing is a little haiku.

Of course, I burst out laughing.

I follow the trail farther into the grove. And there are more drawings on more signs. And more corresponding haikus. Some of them even similar to haikus I just wrote.

It's as if this sacred space is made for me. It's as if I were in a dream. As if manifested from the magic that can only be found amongst the oldest of trees.

Two years ago on that road trip, I found the name Deerfield and became a haikuist. Did I notice these haikus when I stumbled down this trail the first time? Did this place inspire me to write them? Are these haikus mine?

Earth writes its own poetry. We human poets do our best to repeat as much of it back as we can. The longer we go about this process, the further open our hearts grow; someday maybe becoming as wide as the branches of an ancient cedar.

Totally unreal

sometimes landscapes are like paintings

time with **calm brush strokes**.

Temples rise from clouds
seated on these ancient woods
            home of former gods.

            Ice-covered mountains
white brows
      drifting through the fog
lost in time for now.

Triumphant white caps
resting since the dawn of time
      sky is the limit.

I pass Deer House. Deer Lake. Deer Park. Deer Lodge. No Deer Field.

The Montanas turn purple as I drive into them and I'm reminded of how a friend recently asked how I managed to get to heaven. I laugh a little. I told her I just kept driving north.

I didn't find no Santa Claus, but I found pristine mountains covered in glaciers with lakes so reflective it turns the whole world upside down. There are elements like that all over this country, but in Glacier, there is no other thing.

There's a reason they call this God's Country. It's not just because a bunch of loony Bible-thumpers decided to move in sometime in the last century. It's that the gods still live here, alive and well. Sacred places where the Salish, Kootenai, and Blackfeet people celebrated their ancestors for thousands of years.

The only place where all of its natural predators are still healthy, undisturbed by humans.

If I'd been lucky, I would've heard wolves howl.

Read that ranchers are shooting the wolves out of helicopters again in Washington. I signed the petition. Heard that the Shasta pack is still thriving in Northern California after crossing over from Oregon. Watched a documentary about how the wolves, after being reintroduced to Yellowstone, have reshaped the surrounding ecology back to its former glory. Saw that reclaimed beauty for myself, but still wait to hear a wolf's howl.

The Earth sometimes dreams of the days that will lead her to be reunited with the Moon.

Dreams **are
often found
mixed** in with
mountains and
sky

an endless
balance.

I enter Crow Country sometime before midnight. Crow has crawled across the big sky with his feathers blocking out the light. The darkest of nights. I dodge ghosts and other illusions as they jump out at me onto the highway.

Crow hasn't left my side this entire trip. Always Raven on the fence post. Every mile. Like a marker. Each caw with a different dialect. Crow visiting me by the lake. Introducing me to his murder.

Stellar Jay is out there sometimes too. I hear his excited call from the pine forest. He always stands by the places that hold the most magic.

I no longer ask what Crow is saying. I kind of know from experience.

Raven next to Buffalo trying to grab the photographer's attention. Clowning. Hopping around. Calling:

"Hey! Look at me!"

Lakes Whole Lakes taking a break from reading I Ching in the backseat to caw back at him three times. Then four times. Then three times again.

Crow trying to find its partner at Dream Lake, only to attract another. And then another. And then another. And so on. Until there are about fifty crows in the trees all around us doing call and response above while we stare out at the rocky dragon's reflection in the emerald waters. The Clown Baron is the first to say we should head back to the car. Things are starting to look a little too much like Alfred Hitchcock.

I receive a book in Missoula called *The Revolt* from a traveling poet named Walker. On the cover is an illustration of the Raven King. It ends up Walker and I have a lot in common. Travel poets of a similar feather. Eyes for the same roads.

His story reads like *A Sand County Almanac* by Aldo Leopold. The narrative is swept up by what one observes when they refocus their attention to the natural order of things. I find myself reliving so many experiences while I read.

When I leave Crow Country, it's not without some sadness. I have this great feeling that I must return one day soon, paths unfinished.

For now, I head home to Taos. Home of the Gentle Jester Clan. Ravens that laugh from the trees above, and who spend their days slowing time and extending dreams. It's a place unlike anywhere else I've been. A tiny, well-known secret where the healing is in the sky, the water, and the earth. I look forward to what I have left there to learn. To what is left that the place will teach me.

Travel by Haiku

Vol. 10: **Crow Speak For The Moon To The Glaciers.**

with Stephanie Beattie and Cameron Christopher Stuart

Golden
mountain pass

road leads to
uncertainty

pines give up
their ghosts.

The mountains abide

patience forgotten by man

reclaimed in balance.

We drive to
nowhere

*Do Not Approach
the Wild Life*

burn **burn burn**
burn (hide).

Cock logic out West
saddle codpiece rule of thumb
dum dums, trains and grains.

Lobster clouds attack
UFOs in vacant lots
Earth's a pretty place!

Solar sheath his cloud shroud
shimmy crazy in horn-rims
half-eaten point peaks.

This place of
wonder
      time's **illusion**
      pierced **by**
      grandeur

pierced, sapped,
suckle, run dry.

Clouds billow outward
        sifting rain from
    vapor'd chaff
cliffs left **unexposed**.

Lighting is so good
yet *I am so very bad*
you **make bad**
                look good.

Forest **opens wide**

her mossy thighs
stream apart

swooning,
I am found.

We'll **get drunk**
tonight!

Discover a
human peace

mind flows
with the heart.

Another day's hike
      unity of
mind and thought
      foot and mountain trail.

      Chasm in reverse
a break
from **the normal flow**
      clarified in peace.

Potholes in the road

not, chronic,
**filled with
sky-soup**

clowns'
happy
journey.

The rough edge
of speech

will

**manifest
as laughter**

if it **finds its wit**.

Speaking, yet silent

changing leaves
tell the season

dreaming of
winter.

Aspen stands, alone

family cut down
by time
that's one
    tough cowboy!

Father roots spill
you wouldn't **believe it
growing so tall!**

Treetop, no, fog stack
not, appearing yet appears
what does
this all mean?

Ma and two bear cubs
lost horse
      in the wilderness
found berries, lived life.

Pretty orange leaves
 end as **filthy forest loam**
passage to heaven.

Powerful force of
 magical bliss **in order
 by feminine pressure**.

 Fragrance of blossoms
turns stomachs
over wet stumps
 petals stretched from tips.

 It's coming back down
 so yellow and glorious
beneath the red grove.

Road ends,
twelve miles

dead ends
straight into the
ice

so we turn
around.

Night **eclipses thought**

overwhelmed by the moon's rays

words no longer serve.

We travelled
so long

**tickling
curiosity**

till it got

the hiccups.

Tune into Haiku TV:

marshalljameskavanaugh.com/haiku-tv.html

The haikus in this book, when performed live, are accompanied by TV installations and video art. These devices create the atmosphere to experience the space between each line of a haiku. The chapter headers for each section are but a small sampling of the audio/visual components available to you.

Follow the link above to deepen your journey.

Marshall Deerfield is Marshall James Kavanaugh in poetic form. His travels take him to places only the subconscious can sometimes understand.

When he's not on the road he can usually be found in the Philadelphia area with his two cats, building large TV installations.

photo by Jenna Love

Augustus Depenbrock spends his time in Los Angeles puttering around the garden. He imbues his dreams into many objects whether they be words, soil, paint, or stone. It is all a part of the magic to be explored around us.

Shane Donnelly aka Chang Dhan-Ali is an artist and performer who has released numerous albums under the moniker *Many Mansions*. Formerly based in Brooklyn, he now wanders the earth in search of the Stone of the Alchemists.

Tara Lynn Faith Williamson divides her time between heartlands in Boulder, Utah, and along the shores of Lake Atitlán in Guatemala. Her path has led her to study with indigenous teachers in song, dance, and ancestral healing.

Stephanie Beattie is an artist, designer, and editor who specializes in interdisciplinary storytelling. She investigates social and systemic processes via the written word, installed performance, and interactive media.

Cameron Christopher Stuart is a writer and composer. He was born in Florida and now lives in NYC. He often collaborates with various mirror selves, including Seraphic Romance Rots Truth and Glam Wren Stupid Art.

video still by Erica Schreiner

About the Cover

The cover of this book was designed by Marshall James Kavanaugh. The background photo is St. Mary Lake in Glacier National Park, Montana. The lake and glacier-topped peaks emerged after days of fog and clouds.

There's a reason Glacier is called the crown jewel of the American continent.

Other Titles by Marshall James Kavanaugh
Available from A Freedom Books:

. The Sleepers / A Midsummer Day's Dream --- 2012

.. Dream Dialectic: The New Aesthetic --- 2013

... Dream Dialectic: The Little Death --- 2014

.... Fire. Sun. Salutation. --- 2015

..... A-Politico Absurdia --- 2016

...... Travel By Haiku, Volumes 1-5: Still Trippin' Across The States --- 2016

.... Water Is The New Precedent --- 2017

www.afreedombooks.com

Acknowledgements

Thank you to everyone who hosted me along the way in my travels. To my family and to all the friends that I acquired in my journeys across the country.

Special thanks to my editors Lexi Lewis and Erin White for fine-tuning my ramblings and to my dear friend Andrew Galati for his brilliant introduction.

I could not have completed this collection without the support of my patrons. Thank you so much to Melanie Kavanaugh, Karen Kavanaugh, Dana Ross, Gus Depenbrock, Jay Schoen, Kim Frakes, Lisa Mersky, Lance Wyllie, Marian McLaughlin, Oswald Wieser, Maddie DiPasquale, Larry Brownstein, Olga Kilmer, Lindo Yes, Talon Lucas, Marie A. Fritzinger, Lydia Hart, David Roederer, Matt Barrett, Jay Howard, Allie Goldberg, Erin Taylor, Anna Pennington, Sarah Wicker, Mandy Stapleford, Grace Richardson, & Kevin Devaney.

And finally, thanks to Becky Goldschmidt for providing a warm, tea-filled space for this collection to be released.